GW01316388

THE VICTORIANS

Arranged for voices and classroom instruments

Alison and Michael Bagenal

There are four books and cassettes in this series:
Medieval people
Stuart England
Tudor England
The Victorians

Acknowledgements

We are grateful to the following for permission to reproduce photographs: Mary Evans Picture Library, pages 2, 22; Beamish, page 11; The Illustrated London News, pages 27, 28.

We are grateful to the following for permission to reproduce copyright material: B T Batsford Ltd for 'No followers, please!' and 'A pennyworth of fun' from pp 127, 134 *A Ballad History of England* by Roy Palmer (1979); Chappell Music Ltd for 'Washing day' from p 28 *Garners Gay* ed Hamer (1967); Novello & Co Ltd for 'Our shoes are made of leather' from p 16 *Children's Singing Games* ed A B Gomme & C J Sharpe.

We are unable to trace the copyright holder in 'Tatters, the crossing-sweeper's song' from *The Parlour Song Book* ed Michael Turner, and would appreciate any information that would enable us to do so.

Published by the Press Syndicate of the University of Cambridge
The Pitt Building, Trumpington Street, Cambridge CB2 1RP
40 West 20th Street, New York, NY 10011-4211, USA
10 Stamford Road, Oakleigh, Melbourne 3166, Australia

© Longman Group UK Limited 1987
© Cambridge University Press 1996

First published 1987 by Longman Group UK Limited
First published 1996 by Cambridge University Press

Printed in Great Britain by Bell and Bain Ltd, Glasgow

A catalogue record for this book is available from the British Library

Paperback: ISBN 0 521 56947 8
Cassette: ISBN 0 521 56945 1

'The Victorians' cassette contains all the songs and instrumental pieces of this book.

Music in the parlour

Mother plays the pianoforte for some family music.

Won't you buy my pretty flowers?

Voices
Guitar or piano accompaniment

Descant recorders
Xylophone 1 (D,E,F#,G,A,B)
Xylophone 2 (C,D,G)

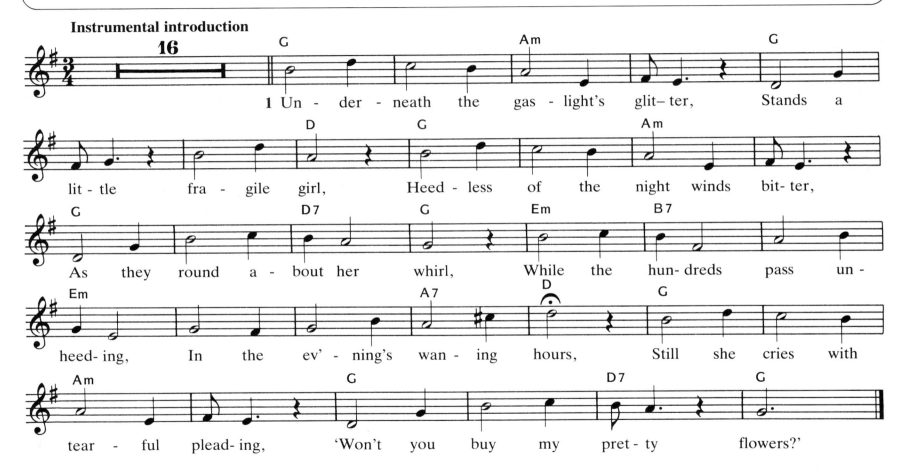

Instrumental introduction

1 Un - der - neath the gas - light's glit- ter, Stands a
lit - tle fra - gile girl, Heed - less of the night winds bit- ter,
As they round a - bout her whirl, While the hun- dreds pass un -
heed- ing, In the ev' - ning's wan - ing hours, Still she cries with
tear - ful plead- ing, 'Won't you buy my pret - ty flowers?'

2 Ever coming, ever going,
Men and women hurry by,
Heedless of the teardrops gleaming
In her sad and wistful eye.

How her little heart is sighing
In the cold and dreary hours;
Only listen to her crying,
'Won't you buy my pretty flowers?'

Chords are suggested for a simple guitar or piano accompaniment, if you wish to use them.

4

Instrumental parts

If you label the notes on your xylophones at the **top** $\boxed{A}$ it is much easier to play the right notes while looking at the music.

Players could copy out their own parts, using large clear staves and coloured pens.

Introduction

For a shorter introduction just play the last four bars.

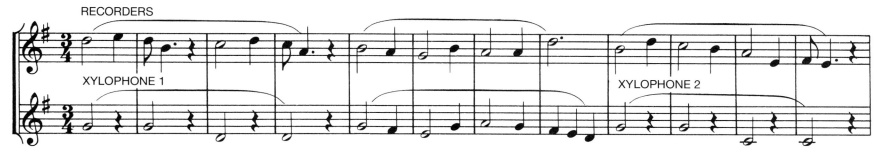

Recorder players now join in the singing of the song, leaving the accompaniment to the two xylophones.

Xylophone accompaniment

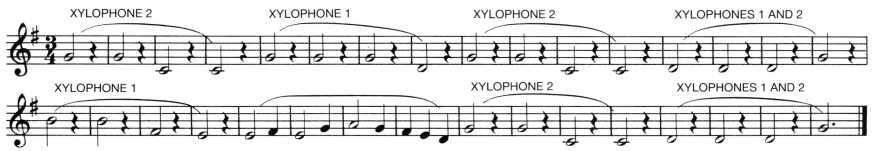

Our shoes are made of leather

a singing game

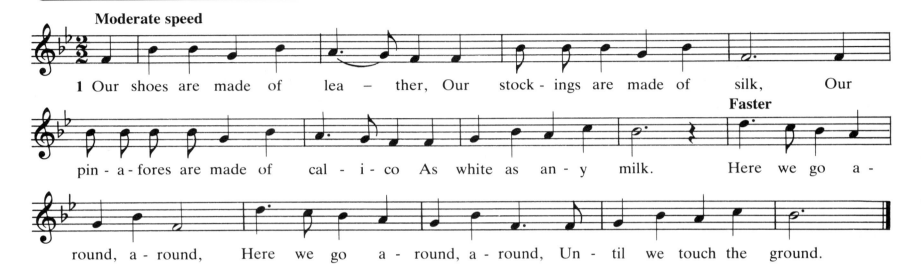

Moderate speed

1 Our shoes are made of lea – ther, Our stock-ings are made of silk, Our

pin-a-fores are made of cal - i - co As white as an - y milk. Here we go a-

Faster

round, a - round, Here we go a - round, a - round, Un - til we touch the ground.

This is a singing game from Somerset for the youngest children in a Victorian family. All stand in a ring, and point, as the song directs, to shoes, stockings, pinafores, etc. For the chorus all join hands and dance round as fast as possible until on the word 'ground' everyone suddenly crouches down.

Here are some more verses. Little boys would wear dresses and pinafores too until they had their first pair of trousers, at six or seven years old.

This song is informal and for voices without accompaniment. Use a xylophone to pitch the first two notes.

2 Our dresses are made of taffeta,
Our sashes are made of silk,
Our slippers are made of finest kid
As white as any milk.

CHORUS Here we go, etc.

3 Our muffs are made of softest fur,
Our bonnets have ribbons of silk,
Our skirts have frills of fine muslin
As white as any milk.

CHORUS Here we go, etc.

The piper o' Dundee

a Scottish march

Descant recorders
Drum
Chime bars

Fine

(Repeat A *)*

Choose a sergeant to give the command 'Forward march! Left. . .left. . .left, right, left!'.

Choose a drummer to set a lively pace:

A Scottish march, something to please the older boys of the family. Queen Victoria became very romantic about Scotland after building her Highland home at Balmoral. Her sons, and many other well-to-do boys, wore kilts and Glengarry caps, and tartan became fashionable.

Accompaniment

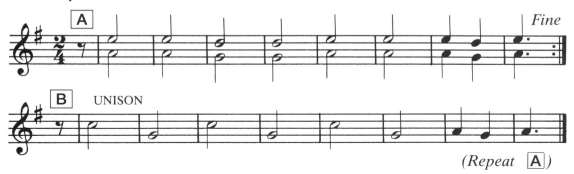

The accompaniment suggests bagpipe drones. Use chime bars, or a metallophone.

(Repeat A *)*

7

Two Victorian hymns

Voices
Simple piano accompaniment

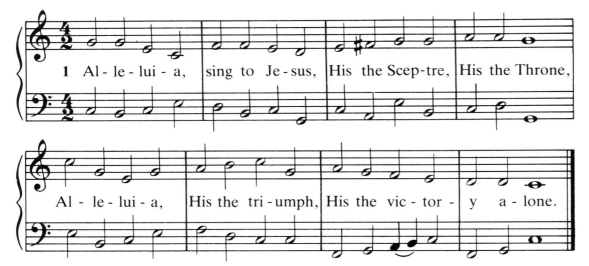

1 Al - le - lui - a, sing to Je - sus, His the Scep - tre, His the Throne,

Al - le - lui - a, His the tri - umph, His the vic - tor - y a - lone.

2 Alleluia, King Eternal,
   Thee the Lord of lords we own,
   Alleluia, Son of Mary,
   Earth Thy footstool,
       Heav'n Thy Throne.

Albert, the Prince Consort, wrote this hymn tune. He was a fine musician and played the organ well. He and Queen Victoria both enjoyed visits from the German composer Mendelssohn, who played to them in the royal music room at Windsor.

An evening hymn

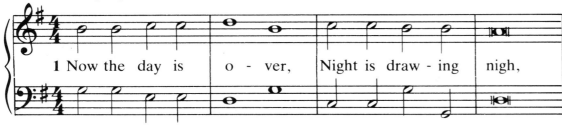

1 Now the day is o - ver, Night is draw - ing nigh,

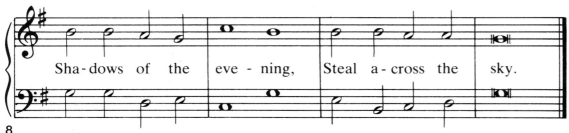

Sha - dows of the eve - ning, Steal a - cross the sky.

2 Now the darkness gathers,
   Stars begin to peep,
   Birds, and beasts, and flowers
   Soon will be asleep.

3 Grant to little children
   Visions bright of Thee;
   Guard the sailors tossing
   On the deep blue sea.

Ideas for using this music

Furnish a corner of the school hall as a **Victorian parlour**. You will want to represent a coal-burning fire and a mantelpiece above it. There should be lots of furniture covered with tablecloths, and plenty of ornaments and potted plants.

Cover the school piano with a decorative cloth too and make it part of your parlour scene. Even if nobody can actually play it, Mama (the mother of your Victorian family) can pretend to!

She and Papa might start a short scene from Victorian family life by sitting by the fire discussing what they have been doing during the day, Papa at his office in the City and Mama running the household, organising the servants' work and making sure the younger children are well looked after by their nurse and nursemaid.

Presently the nursemaid, in cap and apron, might bring in the younger children, followed by the older children. Victorian families tended to be large so there might be five or six children in all. The parents would ask them about their lessons and whether they had been good and obedient. Then the music could begin.

Won't you buy my pretty flowers?

Mama would use this song to teach the children that they should always be kind and pity those who are worse off than themselves. (Modern children might ask 'Is being sorry for people enough?'.)

Our shoes are made of leather

The older girls and the nursemaid would help the younger ones to play this traditional singing game. The older boys would probably stand aside, scornful of such a babyish amusement.

The piper o' Dundee

Papa might step forward now and help the eldest boy to play the sergeant's part and to drill the others. Boys only would be the rule; but they might relent and allow a sister who was 'a good sport' to join in too. All the others will be busy providing the music for marching.

Two Victorian hymns

Music in the parlour would always end with a hymn, especially on Sundays. Parents taught their children to work hard, be grateful for their good homes, say their prayers and behave with respect towards their mother and father.

For a Christmas occasion the following are favourite Victorian hymns; 'Hark, the herald-angels sing', (Mendelssohn's Christmas hymn), 'Once in royal David's city', 'It came upon the midnight clear' and 'Still the night, holy the night'. This is a carol from Germany, and many of our now popular Christmas traditions, like Christmas trees, were introduced to England by Queen Victoria's German husband, Prince Albert.

You might like to play some of the traditional games played at Victorian Christmas parties too, such as 'Blind man's buff', 'Forfeits', and 'Hunt the thimble'. Roast goose and of course plum pudding were the most popular Christmas dishes, with hot punch to keep out the cold, and sweet iced biscuits for the children.

Music below stairs

Parlour maid

Butler

Cook

Housemaid

Laundry maid

Scullery maid

Boot boy

Washing day

or The maid's lament

Voices
Xylophone (C, F, G, top C)
Percussion

The xylophone plays where the music is marked with an 'x'.

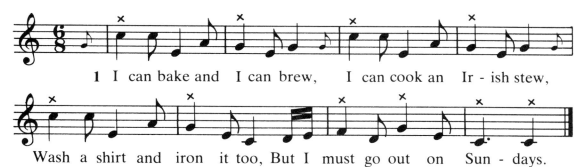

1 I can bake and I can brew, I can cook an Ir - ish stew,

Wash a shirt and iron it too, But I must go out on Sun - days.

2 Six days I work with all my might
   To keep the pots and kettles bright,
   And put the cobwebs out of sight,
   But I must go out on Sundays.

3 I have a young man in the town,
   Some day we hope to settle down,
   Then I shall have a nice new gown,
   But I must go out on Sundays!

Repeat verse 1 to finish the song.

Here is a chorus for all the other servants to sing between verses.

Softly, gradually getting louder and louder

Mon - day, Tues - day, Wed - nes - day, Thurs - day, Fri - day, Sa - tur - day, SUN - DAY!

Try some 'kitchen' percussion effects too like a scrubbing board rasped with a
wooden spoon and pan-lid cymbals.

No followers, please!

or The young man from the country

Voices
Descant recorders
Xylophone

Servant girls were not supposed to entertain their men friends, called 'followers', in the kitchen; this song shows that the rule was sometimes broken, with disastrous results!

1 When first I went to ser - vice a nurse-maid's place I took, There was

me and Jane the house - maid, and Mar - gar - et the cook; We all of us had fol - low - ers, the

best of all the three Was the young man from the count - ry who kept com - pan - y with me!

2 The first time he came in to tea the snow was on the ground,
   Next morning Master's overcoat was nowhere to be found,
   And yet I seed it on the peg, when I sat down to tea
   With that young man from the country who kept company with me.

3 When next he came the dinner things was lying all about,
   For Jane that day was busy, and 'twas Margaret's Sunday out.
   Two silver forks was stole that night, yet no thief did I see,
   No more did that young fellow as kept company with me.

Recorders should play a two-bar introduction, and a short phrase between verses.

Quite a long song, but all five verses are excellent; perhaps an overhead projector could be used for the words.

4 A policeman came for me one day, my evidence to give,
   I never shall forget it the longest day I live,
   I saw in the Old Bailey, condemned for felony
   That young man from the country as kept company with me.

5 'Twas he who stole the forks and spoons, 'twas he the coat as took;
   I lost my place next morning, so did Jane and so did cook!
   Young women all, take warning, don't have followers in to tea,
   Lest they treat you as that young man from the country treated me.

At the very end all shout 'No followers, no followers, NO FOLLOWERS, PLEASE!'

Recorder introduction

During the song the recorders, and possibly a xylophone too, can play this 'skeleton' version of the tune.

The 'skeleton tune' idea can be a useful one for beginners, it gives them just some of the notes to play. It also avoids descant recorders doubling the voices all the way through, which is not a very satisfactory sound.

When first I went to service a nursemaid's place I took, There was me and Jane the housemaid, and Margar - et the cook; We all of us had followers, the best of all the three Was the young man from the country who kept compan - y with me!

Recorders can play either A or B between the verses.

My old man

a music hall song

Voices
Xylophones 1 and 2 (D, F, G, A, C, top D)
Guitar or piano

Xylophone introduction

Label the notes on your xylophones at the top A . This makes them easier to play while you look at the music.

This song needs a robust performance, everyone singing lustily, with hand-clapping and a tambourine to mark the rhythm.

Xylophone accompaniment

Introduction

Both xylophones play the introduction to make it sound loud and cheerful.

Play the xylophone accompaniment on two xylophones playing turn about, four bars each.

XYLOPHONE 1

(My old man said 'Follow the van,)

XYLOPHONE 2

(Don't dilly dally on the way!' ———)

(Off went the cart with the home packed in it,)

(I walked behind with my old cock linnet,)

(dillied and dallied, dallied and dillied,)

(Lost the van and don't know where to roam. ———)

(can't trust the 'specials' like the old-time 'coppers' When you can't find your way home. ———)

can't find your way home. ———)

Ideas for using this music

A domestic servant's life in a large Victorian town house could be very hard; a girl might go into service at the age of ten or eleven and she would be trained strictly by the upper servants. Young boys were employed to clean the boots and shoes or as pages to run errands, and were often called 'Buttons'. The picture on page 10 shows a typical household staff and you can see clearly that some were definitely superior to others. But although life below stairs could be hard there could also be moments of drama and even jollity, as this music shows.

Washing day

Collect as many Victorian household objects as you can, such as a wash-tub, dolly stick (see page 11), flat iron, large kettle, scrubbing board, large pans and wooden spoons. One girl, a young servant in her first job, stands in the midst of these things and complains about all the hard work she has to do, such as carrying cans of hot water upstairs for 'the family' to wash, turning the heavy mangle, washing up piles of dishes in a cold pantry, and so on. Another girl, a more experienced servant, comes to cheer her up, lends a helping hand, and teaches her a song that she learnt from her mother to speed the work along.

As they begin to sing other servants enter, joining in the chorus and playing on 'kitchen' percussion, as suggested below the song text.

No followers, please!

A song for all the servants, but probably not the butler, who would have a room of his own to sit in. I suspect the words of this song are by a professional songwriter bent on amusing his listeners at the girls' expense; not so amusing if you were Jane or cook and lost your place. None of the servants would be given a good reference to help them find another job. And what of the young man himself? Penalties for theft were very severe.

However, I have given the song a rollicking Irish tune, and suggested a noisy ending. The butler would be sure to open the kitchen door and scold the merrymakers, but he might be persuaded to stay and join in singing with them.

My old man

Music halls provided cheap, lively and popular entertainment for people living in Victorian cities. Everyone soon got to know the favourite songs of the day, especially rumbustious ones like this.

The nickname 'copper' for a policeman, someone who catches or 'cops' you, was first used about 1850; other nicknames were 'bobbies' or 'peelers', after Sir Robert Peel who founded the police force. 'Special constables' were appointed to deal with mob riots in Bristol and other large cities in the 1830s.

Mime

The stories of both 'No followers, please!' and 'My old man' could be mimed while the others in the class sing and play instruments. For 'My old man' pile the kitchen furniture onto a table, as the van; you will need a driver with a whip, 'horses', the husband and the young woman, a policeman, and of course a birdcage! Everyone else can dance about while the song is sung a second time.

Off to the park

A nursemaid takes the children for a walk.

Victorian street cries

Voices
Claves or coconut shells

Turkey rhubarb   a traditional song

Don't you all know me, O my name it is Dan, For I am the ce-le-brat-ed Turk-ey rhu - barb man!

Pots and kettles to mend!

Cats' and dogs' meat!

Muffins! New Yorkshire muffins!

Buy my fine myrtles
and roses!

Buy my matches,
my nice small pointed matches!

Some street cries set to music

Toy-sellers

Here's yer toys, for girls or boys!

Pottery-sellers

A-ny earth-en-ware, buy a jug or a tea-pot?

Oyster-men

Oy - sters, new oy - sters! Oy – sters!

Chimney sweeps

Sweeeeeep! Chim-ney swee———p!

On the opposite page you will find more Victorian street cries; you could invent your own tunes for them, and sounds to go with the cries; for example, a bell for the muffin man, cats following the cats' meat man, hammering on metal for the tinker mending kettles.

Why the Turkey rhurbarb man should get his rhubarb from Turkey I don't know, but rhubarb powder was a favourite medicine for stomach upsets.

Set a good rhythm with claves or coconut shells to sound like the clip-clop of horses hooves in the streets:

Divide the singers into four groups; start with the toy-sellers' cry and add the other cries one by one until you have a noisy street scene.

Tatters

the crossing-sweeper's song

Voices
Xylophones (D, E, F#, G, B, E)
Scrapers

Tambourines
Tenor recorders

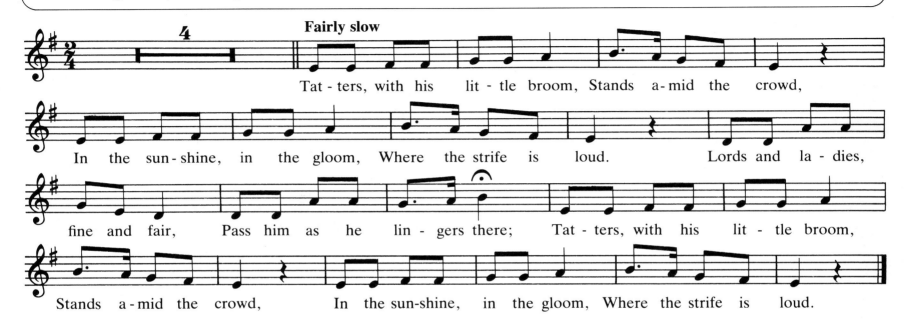

Fairly slow

Tat - ters, with his lit - tle broom, Stands a-mid the crowd,

In the sun-shine, in the gloom, Where the strife is loud. Lords and la - dies,

fine and fair, Pass him as he lin - gers there; Tat - ters, with his lit - tle broom,

Stands a-mid the crowd, In the sun-shine, in the gloom, Where the strife is loud.

Xylophone introduction

Use tambourines and scrapers softly throughout the song to mark the rhythm. Tenor recorders would sound well doubling the voices, or helping the xylophones with the accompaniment.

Xylophone accompaniment

Play [A] twice, [B], then [A] twice again.

A life on the ocean wave

a tune for the band in the park

Xylophones (D, E, G, A, B, top D)
Descant recorders or sopraninos
Mixed percussion

Play at a brisk marching speed

Play ⬜A twice, ⬜B , then ⬜A twice again.

Use drums of all sizes, tambourines, cymbals, and bells; but **not** all at once.

The tune should go at a good marching pace, start quite quietly, and have a marked change of percussion in the ⬜B section, with a rousing final repeat.

A drum introduction will get everyone off to a good start:

Beginner recorders could play the xylophone part. Playing the tune on sopranino recorders will make it sound as if it is being played on military fifes. Begin on G like this:

The xylophone part (G, A, C, D, E) will begin like this:

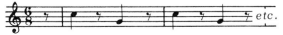

21

Kafoozalum

a polka tune for a barrel organ

Descant recorder 1
Descant recorder 2 (or tenor recorder)
Xylophone (D, G, A)
Tambourine

DESCANT 1

DESCANT 2 OR TENOR RECORDER
XYLOPHONES

Play A, B, A.

The recorders will be making the music while an organ-grinder mimes the turning of the barrel organ handle, so they had better keep out of sight! On page 23 there are some mime ideas to go with this tune.

Beginner recorders could play the xylophone part.

The tambourine marks the rhythm of the polka step – 1, 2, 3, hop!:

Ideas for using this music

Nursemaids would take the younger children in a Victorian family to the park every day, so choose a nursemaid and two children for her to look after. Turn the school hall into a city street scene and the park. As the children and their nursemaid set off for their walk they meet a variety of people:

Street-sellers

The street-sellers would be crying their wares. You could have the Turkey rhubarb man reappear and repeat his song to link the different episodes of this section together. It makes an effective street scene if you have some cries shouted and some sung. The children would be interested in the things for sale and want to linger perhaps by the tinker mending pots and pans, but the nursemaid would hurry them on.

Crossing-sweeper   (Tatters)

The children and nursemaid would be sure to see a crossing-sweeper with his broom. Victorian streets could be very muddy and ladies would not want to get their long skirts dirty. Crossing-sweeper boys earned a few pence sweeping the cobbles so that the gentry could cross cleanly. Interrupt the noisy street cries for Tatters' song.

The band   (A life on the ocean wave).

Arriving at the park, the nursemaid and children would enjoy listening to the band playing 'A life on the ocean wave'. This tune is the official march of the Royal Marines. You will need a smart bandmaster to beat time. The accompaniment sounds like the 'oompah' section of a brass band; four or five bandsmen could stand by the xylophones and mime the playing of trombones and tubas.

Organ-grinder   (Kafoozalum)

On their way home the nursemaid and children come upon an organ-grinder playing a barrel organ in the street. He would probably have been an Italian, and wear a colourful handkerchief round his neck, perhaps you could give him curled mustachios too. His barrel organ can be a grocer's box painted with bright colours and carried by straps over his shoulders, and he will need to pretend to turn a handle on its side to work the mechanical music cylinder inside the box. Often organ-grinders had a pet monkey who perched on the organ or took round a tin mug for money. You might use a toy monkey; or a small boy or girl might like to scamper about with the tin mug among the dancers.

Muffin man

Finally, the nursemaid might buy some muffins from the muffin man to take home for nursery tea.

Poverty, hardship, and adventure

A soldier and sailor on leave

The new poor law

a poem to recite with improvised music and mime

1   Success to old England, with peace, trade, and plenty,
    Of good meat abundance, and all kinds of dainty,
    The grain is well housed, with plenty in store,
    Yet rich men are griping and grinding the poor.

2   Suppose a poor man no employment can find;
    The parish relief is both cruel and unkind.
    He'll be starving for food, hard at labour all day –
    Cold charity, this, from the workhouse, I'd say.

3   A poor couple may have children one, two, or three,
    They'll be ta'en from their parents, no daylight to see;
    Still more than all this, which will cause grief and strife,
    A man must be parted from his own loving wife.

4   Now cometh sharp winter when the weather is cold,
    How piercing it seems to the sick and the old;
    All those who have thousands they still cry for more,
    All you have plenty, remember the poor.

5   Now for to conclude these few lines which I've penn'd
    May the rich to the poor man still yet prove a friend,
    The new poor law bill, let it be cast away,
    Abolish the workhouse for ever, I say!

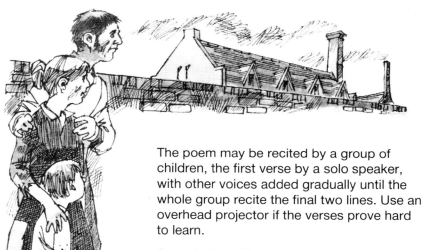

The poem may be recited by a group of children, the first verse by a solo speaker, with other voices added gradually until the whole group recite the final two lines. Use an overhead projector if the verses prove hard to learn.

A musical backing may be built up in the same way, using xylophones, glockenspiels and chime bars. Ask the children to experiment with the following notes C, D, E, G, A, with A as the home note, making up their own note patterns and rhythms (ostinatos) to suit the words. It would be best to start with one solo instrument; add violins, guitars or other percussion effects, for example, cymbals tapped with a padded stick. The backing should basically be soft and follow the words carefully (shivering sounds for 'Now cometh sharp winter'). The music, like the words, should rise to a final climax.

See page 32 for mime ideas to go with this poem.

These verses are taken from a song about the new poor law of 1834. It was a harsh law; anyone who was unable to work and so driven to beg for charity, or 'relief', from their parish had to go to the workhouse to labour for their meagre rations and comfortless shelter there. Husbands, wives and children were separated. This was to discourage the poor from seeking parish relief; the workhouse became so dreaded people would rather starve than go there.

Polly Parker, a poor collier lass

Voices
Xylophones 1 and 2 (C, D, E, G, A, top D)

Xylophone introduction
Both xylophones play the introduction.

Moderate speed

1 My name's Pol-ly Par-ker, I come o - ver from Wor-ley, —— My fath-er and moth-er work in the coal - mine, —— Our fam - i - ly's large, we have

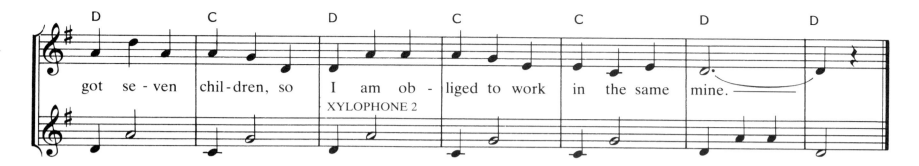

got se-ven chil-dren, so I am ob-liged to work in the same mine.

XYLOPHONE 2

2 By the greatest of dangers each day I'm surrounded,
I hang in the air by a rope or a chain,
The mine may fall in, I may be killed or wounded
May perish by damp or the fire of the *train.

3 All the day long you may say we are buried,
Deprived of the light and the warmth of the sun,
And often at night from our beds we are hurried
The water is in, and bare footed we run.

Repeat verse 1 to finish.

*train = trail of gunpowder

The song is nominally in D but C♮ is used
throughout.

Guitar chords: tune the bottom E down
to D and play three lowest strings for D,
barré them for E, play a single open
string for G, C chord as normal.

Johnny Todd

or The Liverpool sands, a folk song.

Descant recorders 1 and 2
Voices

Liverpool was the most important trading centre for cotton in Victorian England.

Try a spoken backing to this music. 'Liverpool sands' spoken quietly four times can introduce the music:

Liv-er-pool sands

then add gradually the names of different places to which ships from Liverpool would sail: New York, Canada, Ireland, Australia, Capetown, Brazil, and so on. Speak the words quietly to match the rhythm of the melody. Speakers might sit in groups and choose their own words. Taper the voices off gradually to silence when the music comes to an end.

The rambling soldier

an old soldier's song

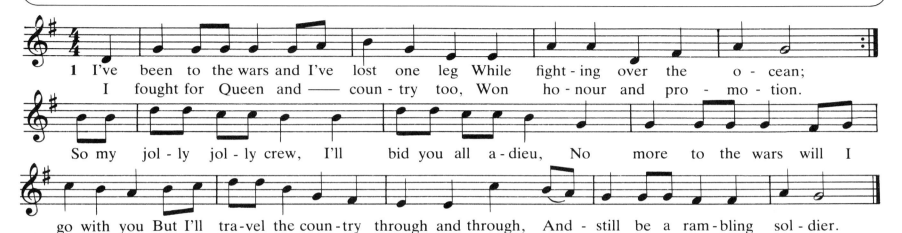

1 I've been to the wars and I've lost one leg While fight-ing over the o-cean;
I fought for Queen and —— coun-try too, Won ho-nour and pro-mo-tion.
So my jol-ly jol-ly crew, I'll bid you all a-dieu, No more to the wars will I
go with you But I'll tra-vel the coun-try through and through, And-still be a ram-bling sol-dier.

2 And if anybody here wants to know my name,
My name it is Ben Johnson,
I have a message from my mates
To court all the girls that are handsome;
To court 'em all both old and young,
To court 'em all and marry none,
To court 'em all and marry marry none,
And still be a rambling soldier!

Keep the following drum rhythm steady throughout:

A 'descant' for recorders to play at the end of each line of the song.

29

A pennyworth of fun

or Riding on the Oxford railway, opened 1852

Voices
Tenor recorders
Percussion
Xylophone

1 If you will list - en to my song, I'll not de - tain you ver - y long. On the

first of May the folks did throng To view the Ox - ford rail - way And have a ride, O

what a treat, Fa - ther, mo - ther son and daugh-ter, A - long the line like one o'- clock By

CHORUS

fire and steam and wa - ter. Ri - fum, ti - fum, mirth and fun, Don't you won - der

how it's done? Car - ria-ges with - out hor - ses run A - long the Ox - ford rail - way.

30

2 When it's finished at both ends
You may send your cocks and hens
And go and visit all your friends
With ducks and pigs and turkeys.
To any part wherever you please
You may send your butter and eggs
And they can ride who've got no legs
Along the Oxford railway.

Rifum, tifum, etc.

Keep the following percussion rhythm going throughout:

Accompaniment for tenor recorders (and xylophone)

Ideas for using this music

This is a collection of tunes related to some of the many aspects of life in Queen Victoria's reign. To present them in a single dramatic episode would be difficult, but they each tell us by their words and by their tunes, cheerful or sad, how people lived, and help us to enter into the Victorian world. You may wish to link one or two of them with the other sections of this book, for example, 'The rambling soldier' might be sung sitting on a park bench!

The new poor law
This is a traditional or folk song; I have added verse 2 to illustrate what workhouse life might mean for the very poor. Any study of nineteenth century Britain is sure to highlight the great difference between the rich and the poor. Why were such cruel laws passed?

The song provides an opportunity for improvised music and mime. While the verses are spoken, men, women and children may enter and mime the workhouse tasks; grinding pulses, pulling hemp, sweeping, scrubbing, etc.

Polly Parker, a poor collier lass
The lives of children working in the coalmines were pitiful in the extreme. The song describes most vividly some of the dreadful dangers the children faced, and the modal tune expresses the sad and helpless feelings of the singer.

Johnny Todd, or the Liverpool sands, a folk song
Many thousands of Irish immigrants landed at Liverpool docks during Queen Victoria's reign, and many thousands of men, women and children left England also to settle in America and the Colonies.

Before putting the spoken part of this tune together you might make a large map of the world as it was at the end of the century, with the British Empire coloured red. Mark in too the most important trade routes and ports of call for trading vessels from Liverpool.

The rambling soldier, an old soldier's song
This is a cheerful campfire song making light of the soldier's life of hardship. The story of the Crimean War makes it clear that soldiers had little to be cheerful about in that campaign. Perhaps this soldier was lucky enough to be nursed back to health by Florence Nightingale.

A pennyworth of fun or Riding on the Oxford railway
Railways brought about great changes in Victorian life, and caused greater financial and social excitement.

This song calls for the miming of pistons, crank shafts and wheels while it is sung, and a whistle sounding off between verses (get four recorder players to play F#, A, B, and top D as a chord), and use percussion to keep the rhythm going.